# Simple Maths

# Subtracting and Taking Away

### Richard Leffingwell

**www.raintreepublishers.co.uk**
Visit our website to find out more information about **Raintree** books.

To order:
 Phone 44 (0) 1865 888112
 Send a fax to 44 (0) 1865 314091
 Visit the Raintree Bookshop at **www.raintreepublishers.co.uk** to browse our catalogue and order online.

First published in Great Britain by Raintree, Halley Court, Jordan Hill, Oxford OX2 8EJ, part of Harcourt Education.
Raintree is a registered trademark of Harcourt Education Ltd.

© Harcourt Education Ltd 2006
First published in paperback in 2007
The moral right of the proprietor has been asserted.

Editorial: Diyan Leake and Cassie Mayer
Design: Joanna Hinton-Malivoire and
  The Partnership
Picture Research: Erica Newbery
Production: Duncan Gilbert

Originated by Modern Age
Printed and bound in China by
  South China Printing Company

10 digit ISBN 1 4062 0391 2 (hardback)
13 digit ISBN 978 1 4062 0391 2
10 09 08 07 06
10 9 8 7 6 5 4 3 2 1

10 digit ISBN 1 4062 0396 3 (paperback)
13 digit ISBN 978 1 4062 0396 7
11 10 09 08 07
10 9 8 7 6 5 4 3 2 1

**British Library Cataloguing in Publication Data**
Leffingwell, Richard
Subtracting and Taking Away
513.2'12
A full catalogue record for this book is available from the British Library.

**Acknowledgements**
The publishers would like to thank the following for permission to reproduce photographs: Alamy pp. **14**, **15**, **16**; Getty Images (Photodisc Red/Davies & Starr) pp. **5**, **6**, **7**, **8**; Harcourt Education Ltd (www.mmstudios.co.uk) pp. **4**, **9–12**, **17–22**, back cover

Cover photographs reproduced with permission of Photolibrary (Brand X/Burke Triolo) and Jupiter Images (FoodPix).

The publishers would like to thank Patti Barber, Specialist in Early Childhood and Primary Education, Institute of Education, University of London, for her assistance in the preparation of this book.

Every effort has been made to contact copyright holders of any material reproduced in this book. Any omissions will be rectified in subsequent printings if notice is given to the publishers.

The paper used to print this book comes from sustainable resources.

# Contents

# What is subtracting?

Subtracting can help you find out how many things you have left.

Subtracting is useful in many ways.

# Subtracting shells

Pretend that you have 5 shells.

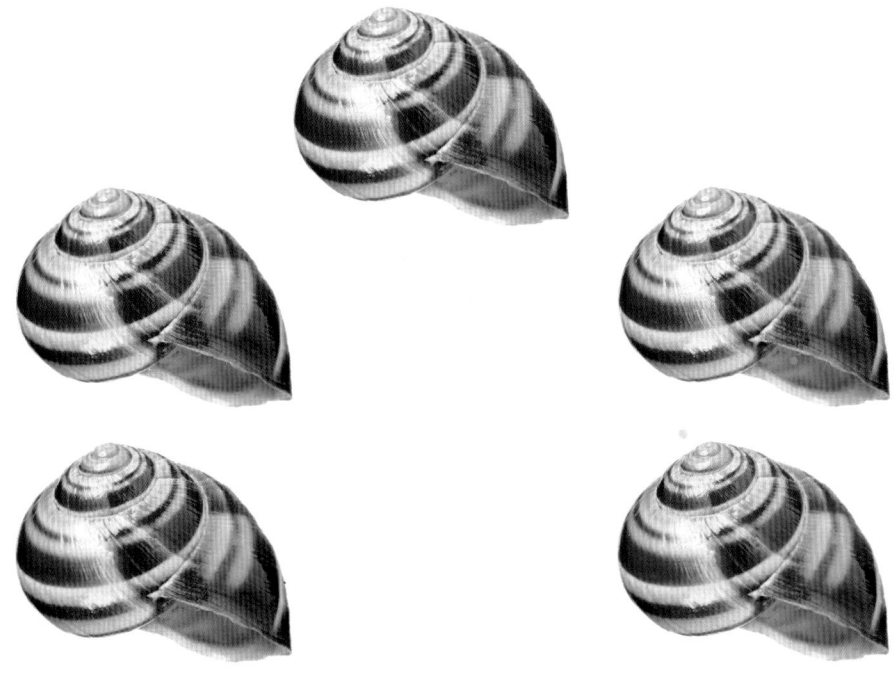

You take 2 shells and give them to a friend.

5 − 2 = ?

How many shells do you have now?

Take away 2 shells from the group of 5.

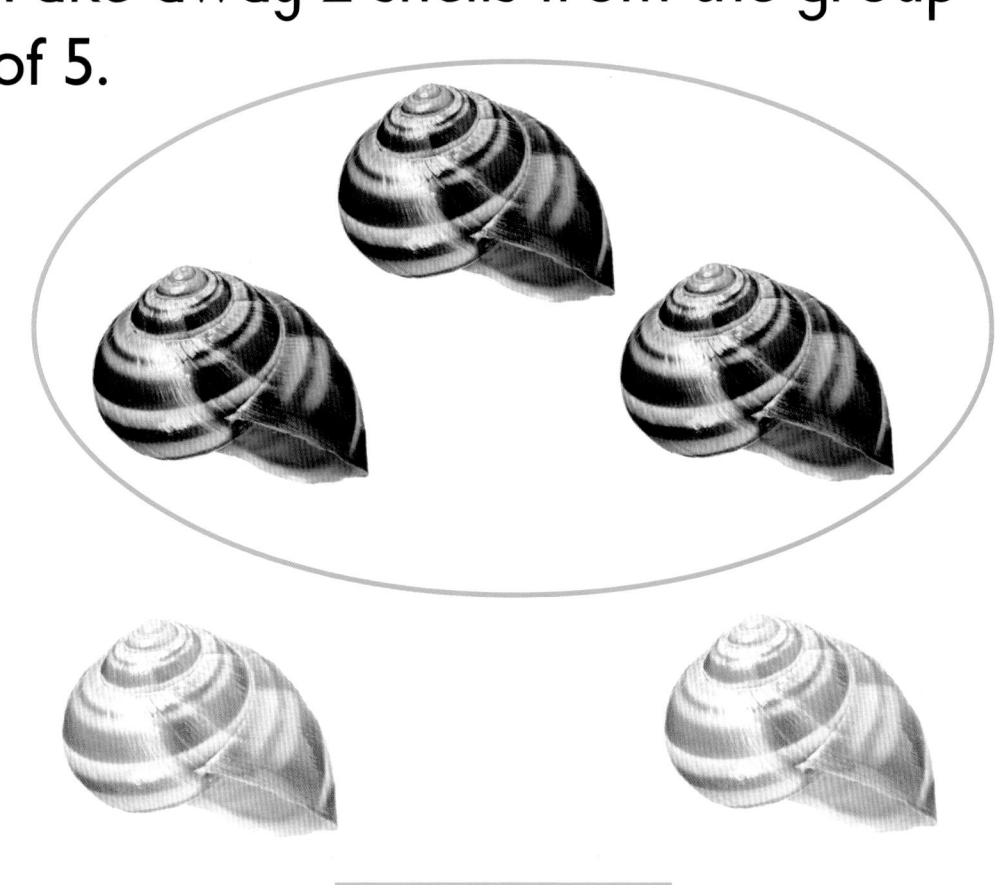

5 − 2 = 3

Now count to see how many you have left.

There are 3 left.

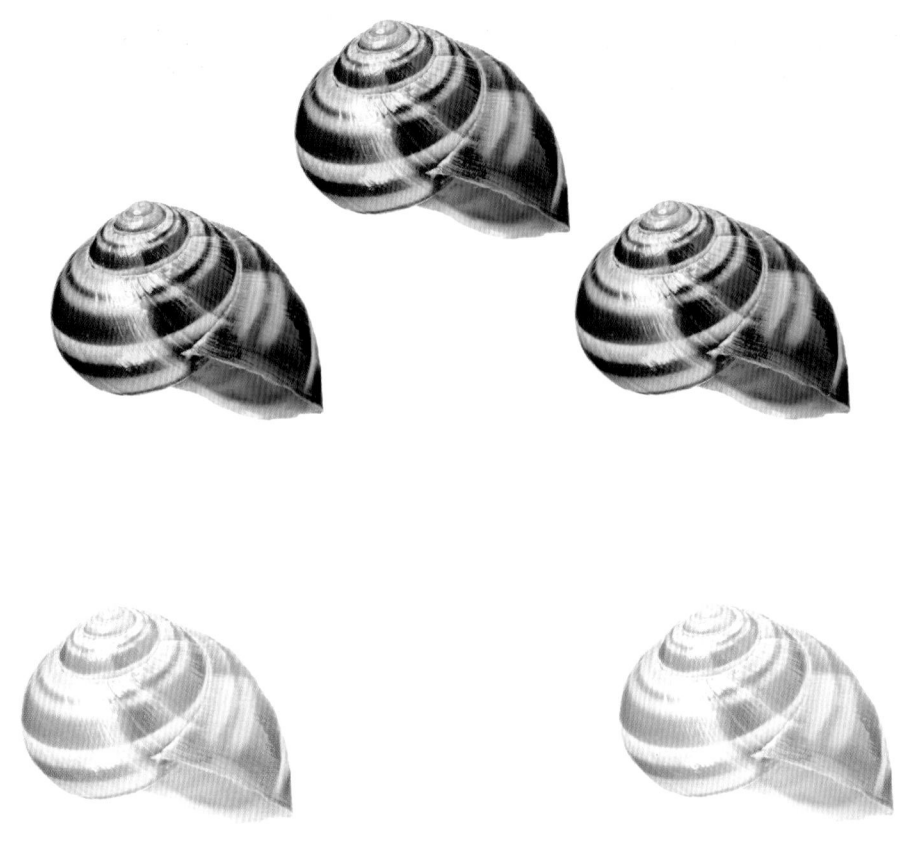

When you take away items from a
group, you are subtracting them.

# Subtracting stones

$$6 - 2 = ?$$

Pretend that you have 6 stones and give 2 of them away.

How can you find out how many are left?

You can draw a picture and count the stones.

$$6 - 2 = 4$$

You have 4 left.

How else can you find out how many are left?

You can count back.

Count back once for each stone that was taken away.

Start counting back from 6.

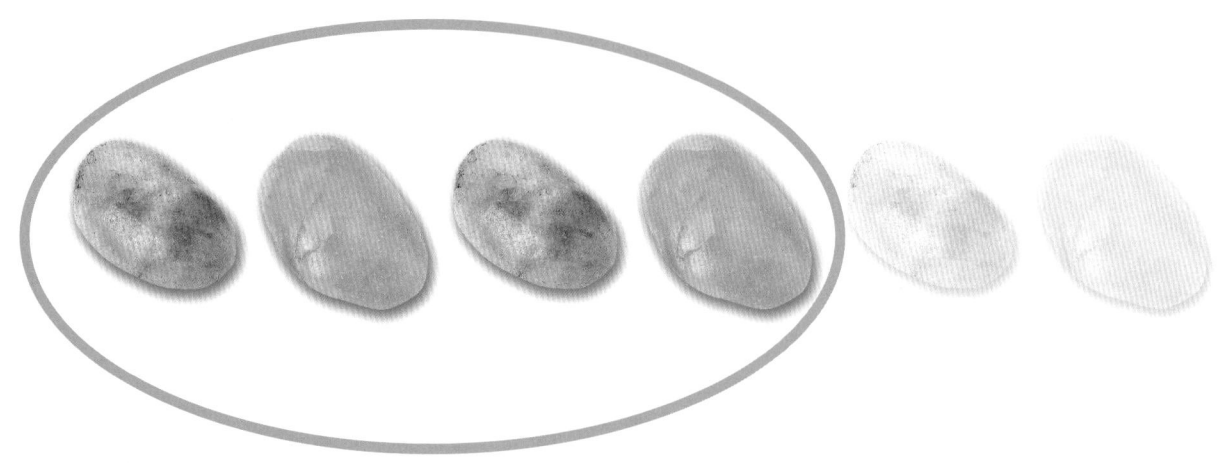

$$6 - 2 = 4$$

You took away 2 stones.

You have 4 stones left.

1   2   3   4   5   6

$$6 - 2 = 4$$

Counting back is when you count backwards from the number you started with.

You count back once for each thing that is taken away.

# Subtracting leaves

Pretend that you have 4 leaves and give 1 away.

Find out how many leaves you have by counting back.

You started with 4 leaves.

Count back from 4.

Count back 1 time.

Count back for each leaf that is taken away.

You counted back 1 time.

You have 3 leaves left.

# Comparing groups

Pretend that you have 5 pencils.

Your friend has 3 pencils.

How many more pencils do you have?

To solve the problem, compare the two groups.

When you compare two groups, you are subtracting.

Look at the two groups.

$$5 - 3 = ?$$

Can you see how many more pencils
there are in your group?

You can see that 5 is 2 more than 3.

5 − 3 = 2

You have 2 more pencils.

Subtraction helps you find out how many of something is left.

$$8 - 2 = ?$$

You also subtract when you compare two groups.

That way you find out how many more there are in the bigger group.

$$3 - 1 = ?$$

# Quiz

Can you work out how many more red pencils there are?

Hint: Use the number line to count back.

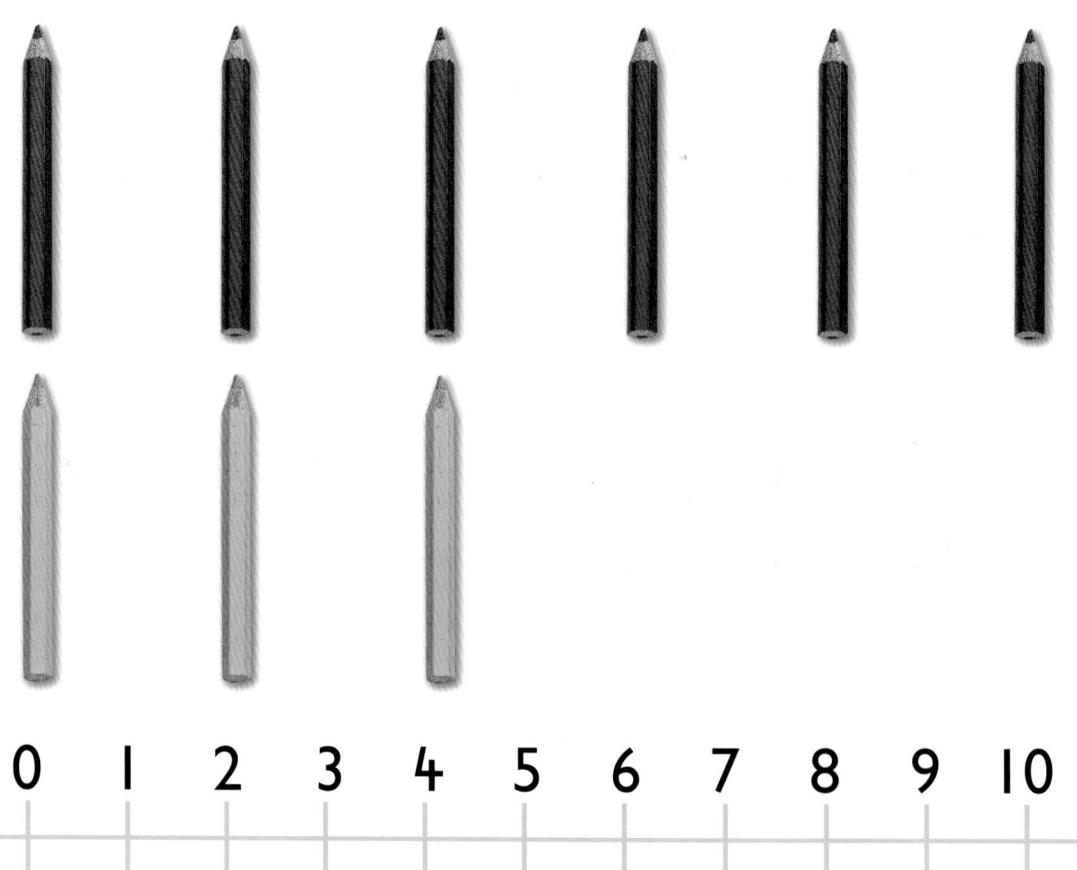

0  1  2  3  4  5  6  7  8  9  10

# The minus sign

| − | You use this sign to show that you are taking one number away from another. |

$$3 - 2$$

When you take 2 away from 3, you get 1.

| = | You use the equals sign to show what 3 minus 2 is equal to. |

$$3 - 2 = 1$$

# Index

**Answer to the quiz on page 22**
There are 3 more red pencils.

**Note to parents and teachers**

Reading non-fiction texts for information is an important part of a child's literacy development. Readers can be encouraged to ask simple questions and then use the text to find the answers. Most chapters in this book begin with a question. Read the questions together. Look at the pictures. Talk about what the answer might be. Then read the text to find out if your predictions were correct. To develop readers' enquiry skills, encourage them to think of other questions they might ask about the topic. Discuss where you could find the answers. Assist children in using the contents page, picture glossary and index to practise research skills and new vocabulary.